Balloon Sculpting

Best Simple Animal Patterns for Twisting Balloon

TABLE OF CONTENT

INTRODUCTION   3

BALLOON TWISTING FROM SCRATCH A - WHICH BALLOONS TO USE?   4

PATTERN 1 - THE DOGGY   8

PATTERN 2 - THE FROG   25

PATTERN 3 – THE TIGER   42

PATTERN 4 - TUX THE PENGUIN   59

PATTERN 5 - THE GIRAFFE   76

Introduction

Knowing how to make balloon animals is a great skill for entertaining children. Whether you are a parent, magician, clown, or healthcare worker, you can delight kids with your custom creations. Learn how to get started as a beginner with the instructions below, which include the types of balloons to use, basic techniques, and step-by-step tutorials for easy balloon animals.

Balloon Twisting From Scratch
A - Which Balloons To Use?

You purchased a beginner's kit with the following contents : a hand pump, a set of instructions and... a number of what appears to be twisting balloons.

Now, you expectantly imagine the happiness and fun you will bring to your child's birthday party and decide to practice a little bit ahead of time. Following the instructions, you start inflating the balloon but - bad luck, surely - it blows up with a loud pop!!

Hmm... after a deep breath, you start inflating another balloon again, this time a little more slowly and carefully and... with success.

Triumphantly, you undertake the knot but - bad luck, surely - it pops again.

But you are not one to be easily discouraged, so you try again (and again.. and again... and...) until finally you succeed in tying the knot (of the balloon). Delving back into the instructions, you start twisting your very first bubble and - bad luck, surely - it pops again.

You reach towards the balloons, and it is then you realize with horrified dismay that the whole pack is nearly gone and you only have 3 balloons left for your child's party.

To make a long story short, you end up utterly frustrated and you quit in despair being fully persuaded that balloon twisting is not for you and that only a very special kind of people can actually do it.

But guess what ? You simply did not have the right balloon. Yes, you heard correctly, you didn't have the right balloons!

I know, it's hard to believe that these lovely balloon kits sell with crummy balloons. But sadly, that seems to be the norm and the reason is simply mercantile; crummy balloons, or crummy anything for that matter, will always be cheaper to manufacture than quality ones.

There are actually very few companies manufacturing good quality twisting balloons.

The world leader is Qualatex. Qualatex offers an incredible array of balloons in all kinds of shapes, colors and sizes, and not only for modeling.

And a close contender here in Europe is Sempertex who also offers a wide array of balloons, notably the original link-o-loon balloons that can be attached from both sides. But I digress.

Modeling balloons are identified by their diameter and by their length: 160, 260, 321, 350, 360, 646, 660, etc. The first number matching the diameter while the two others match the length.

In other words:

- 160 represents a twisting balloon, fully blown, measuring 1 inch wide and 60 inches long.
- 260 represents a twisting balloon, fully blown, measuring 2 inches wide and 60 inches long.
- 350 represents a twisting balloon, fully blown, measuring 3 inches wide and 50 inches long.

And so on, and so forth.

A beginner will usually concern himself only with 260's to start with.

If these 2 brands of balloons are not always sold in brick and mortar shops, you can find and buy them easily on Internet.

One word of caution though... until you gain more experience, stay away from transparent colors which are a bit more fragile. For a start, you may prefer the standard or fashion colors.

Pattern 1 - The Doggy

Step-By-Step Photo Guide

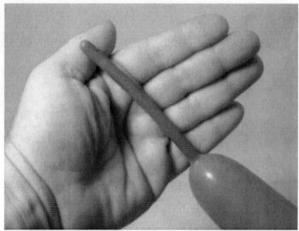

1- Inflate a balloon leaving a margin at the end of about the width of a hand. Then tie a knot without making it too tight.

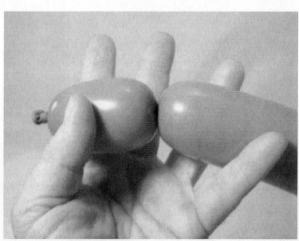

2- Starting from the knotted end, make a first bubble about three fingers wide at most. This will be the dog's head.

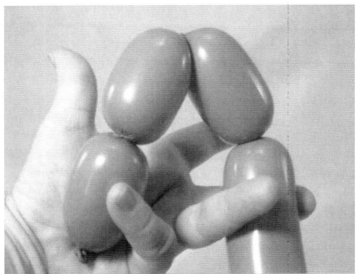

3- Make two more bubbles following it, of the same size as the first. These will be its two ears.

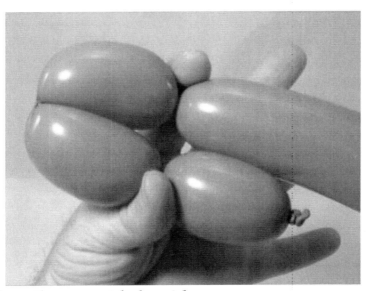

4- Place the ears side by side.

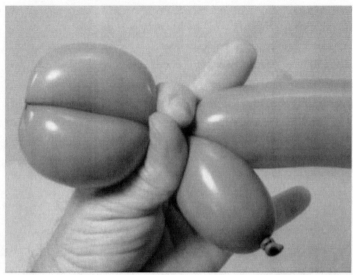

5- Press two fingers at their base to pinch both folds together...

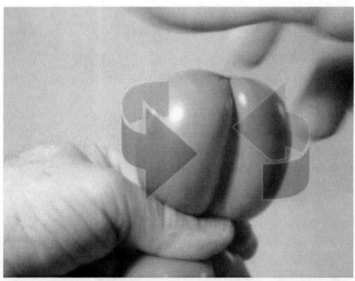

6- and with your other hand, twist both ears ears together around their base several times to keep them in place.

7- Two ears appear, pointing straight up on top of the dog's head. This is the simplest version of the iconic balloon dog.

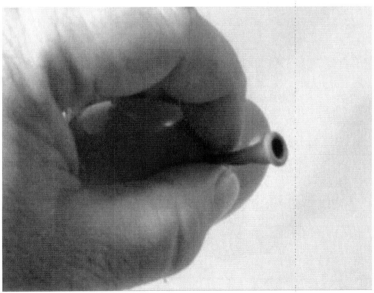

8- To make a dog with floppy ears, hold the knot with one hand...

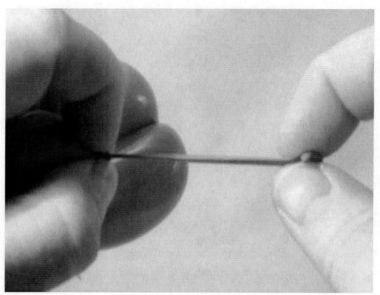

9- then, with the other hand, pull on the nozzle while keeping the knot firmly pinched, to free up an extra length of balloon.

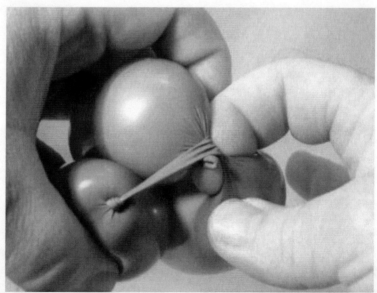

10- Pull the nozzle under the fold at the **bottom** of the ears...

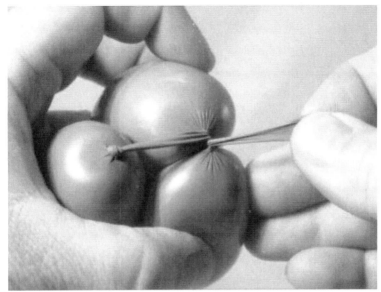

11- take it from the other side of the fold and stretch the length of balloon further.

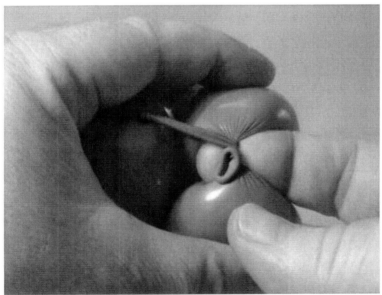

12- Roll the nozzle around this fold again in the same way at least two or three more times.

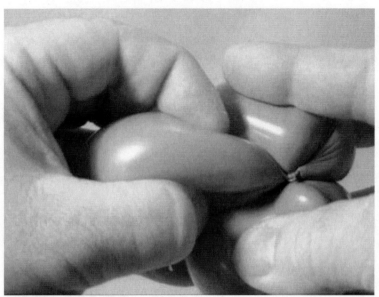

13- Next, turn around the dog's head and pull apart the **top** of the two bubbles forming the ears, to wedge in the **top** of the head bubble.

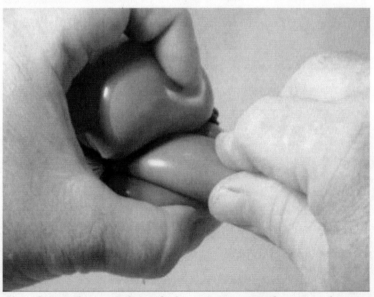

14- On the other side of the ears, wedge in the top of the remaining portion of balloon in the same way.

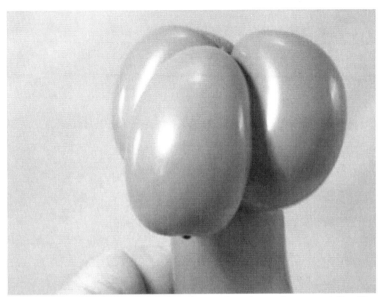

15- Like this, you get the head of a dog with floppy ears.

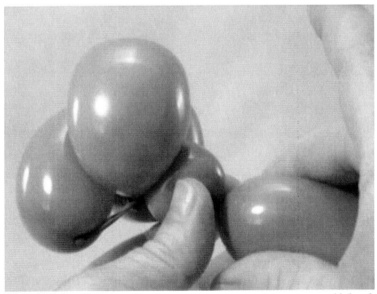

16- To shape the neck, be sure to make a small bubble. Don't make it too big, this isn't a giraffe!

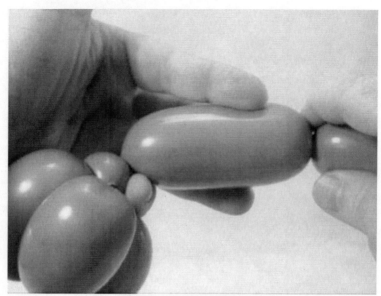

17- Hold the head well so the neck bubble doesn't escape, and shape the first front leg.

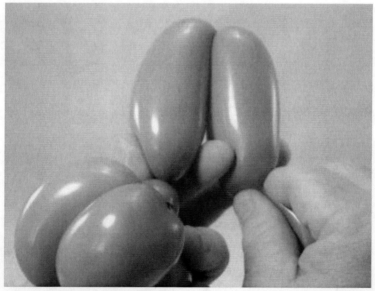

18- Then, shape the second front leg, making sure it's the same size as the first one.

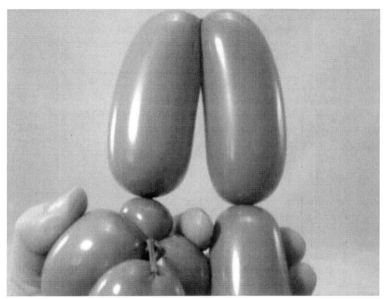

19- Bring the two legs together...

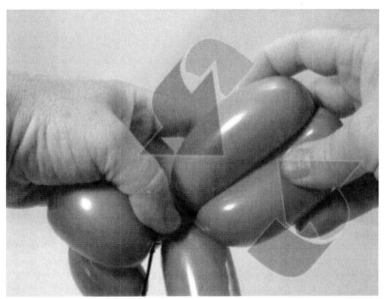

20- then, as for the ears, press the base of both bubbles together, and twist them together several times to block them together.

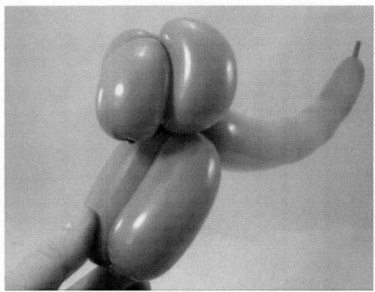

21- If need be, rearrange each part so that the doggy's head and front legs are facing in the right direction.

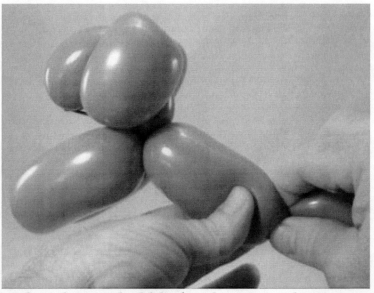

22- Make a longer bubble for the stomach.

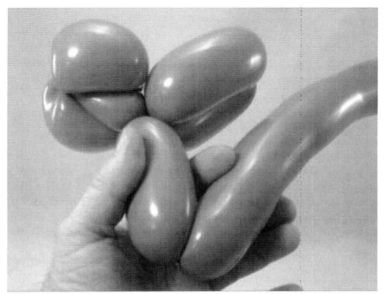

23- To make the first hind leg, place the remaining portion of balloon parallel to the front legs...

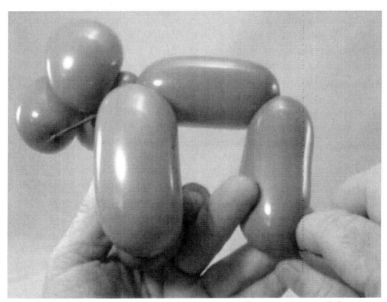

24- so that it's easier to compare their size. Obviously, they need to be roughly the same length.

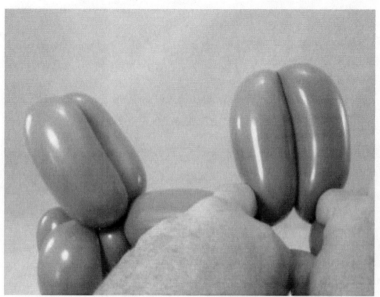

25- You also need to check that the second hind leg is the same length as the first one.

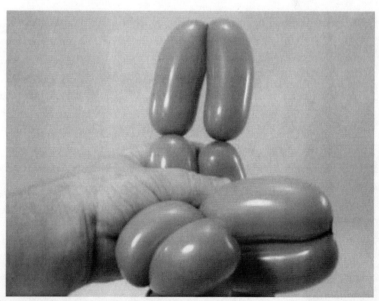

26- As for the ears and the front legs, bring the hind legs close together...

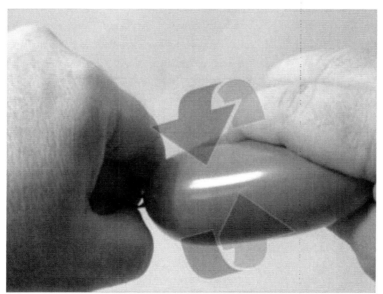

27- press their base and twist both bubbles together to block the hind legs together.

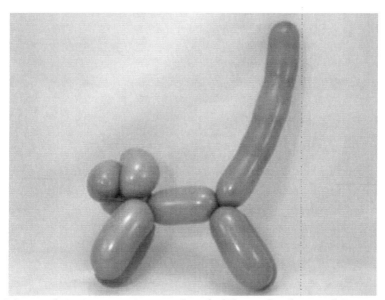

28- Now this is starting to look like a little and improve a few details for our dog to be less stiff and more natural-looking.

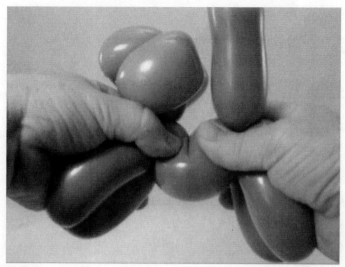

29- Hold both ends of the stomach bubble and gently move them back and forth, to rub them gently against each other at the center of the bubble.

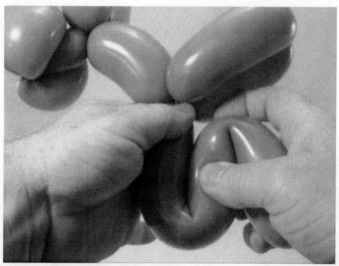

30- Next, press the tail bubble between your hands, to form an **S** shape, and like previously, rub gently at the folds of the S.

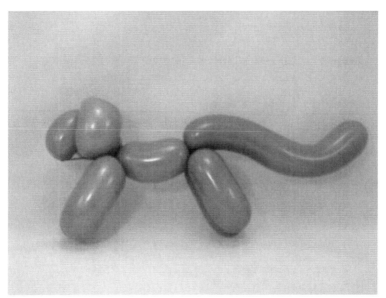

31- Have a little dog with much more natural and nice-looking curves.

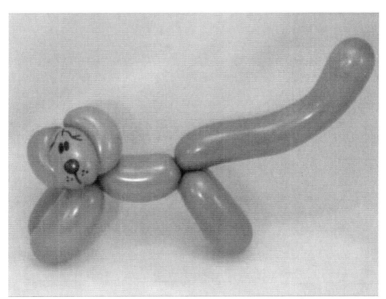

32- Draw a few features on the dog to bring it to life.

33- Alternatively, to get a shorter tail, make the legs longer.

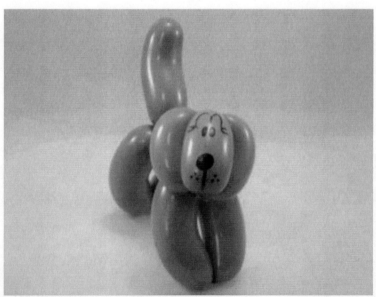

34- The result!

Pattern 2 - The Frog

Recommendation:

- Are all the bubbles for the frog's eyes round and the same size? Or are they too long, or unequal?

- Are the bubbles for the front legs well-proportioned and small enough? Or are they too big and difficult to fit into the hind legs, which are now too small because there wasn't really enough length remaining to make them appropriately.

- Have the segments for the two hind legs been formed into two, long, separate bubbles? Or have they inexplicably been replaced by a single loop? What is the loop even meant to represent? Nobody knows.

- Have the eyes been drawn widely enough? Or are they just simple black dots, almost impossible to make out?

- Is the curve of the mouth drawn as a wave that's upturned at each end and takes up most of the available surface? Or is it just some kind of tiny semi-circle? (**Tip:** Take a sheet of rough paper, and practice drawing the curve in a single stroke, several dozen times if you have to, before trying it again on the balloon)

Step-By-Step Photo Guide

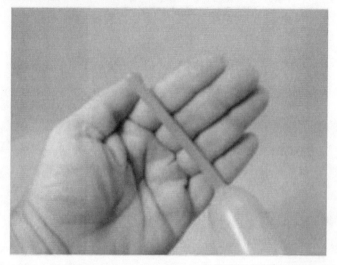

1- Inflate a balloon leaving a margin at the end of about the width of a hand, then tie a knot without making it too tight.

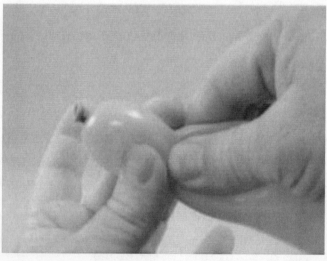

2- Starting from the knotted end, make a first, well-rounded bubble, about two fingers wide at most.

3- Make three more bubbles following it, of the same size as the first.

4- Pull the knot of the balloon and hold it to the base of the four bubbles...

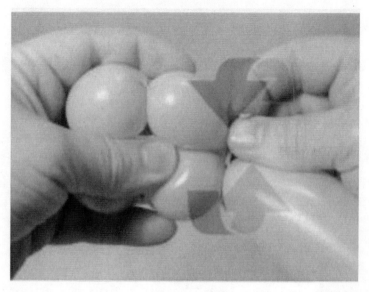

5- then twist all four bubbles together several times, while holding the knot to their base, to block the assembly together.

6- The result should look like this.

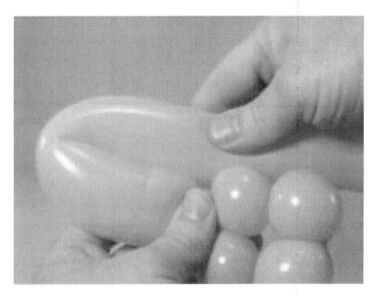

7- Fold the balloon at a length that's slightly larger than the height of the four bubbles to form a loop.

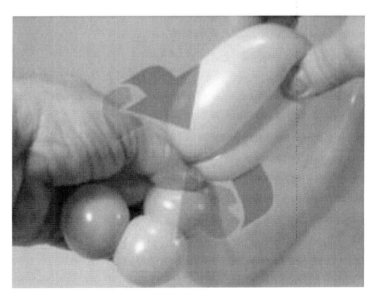

8- Block the loop at the base of the bubbles.

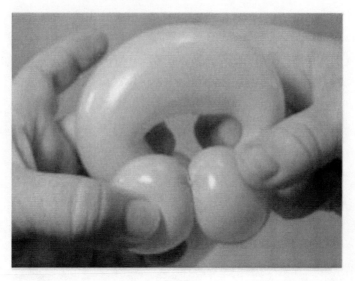

9- Open the loop wide with your middle fingers and place your thumbs on each of the top bubbles.

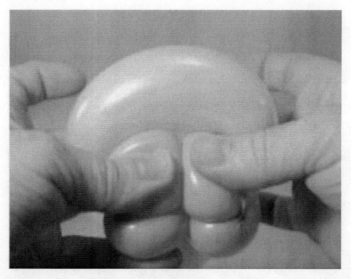

10- Press the two top bubbles making a clamp movement towards the inside of the loop, still held firmly with your middle fingers.

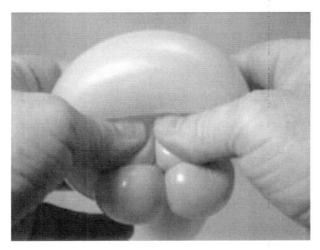

11- Push the two top bubbles all the way into the loop, pressing in increments so that the friction on the lining of the balloon isn't too high.

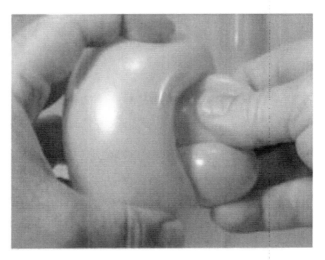

12- Once the two top bubbles come out on the other side of the loop, take hold of them and finish embedding them on the other side of the loop. (Careful: Don't push the bottom bubbles through at the same time!)

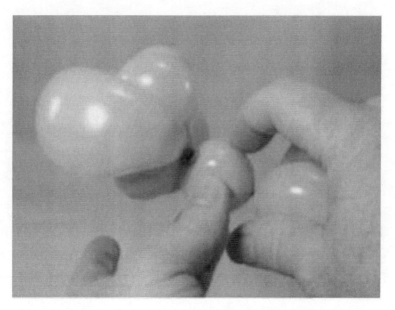

13- Then form a little, well-rounded bubble...

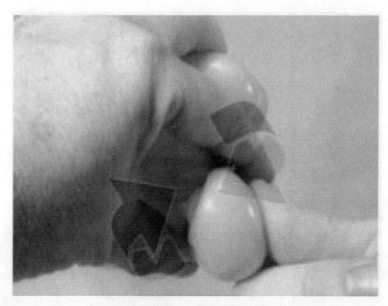

14- and make that bubble into a "pinch-twist"

15- The result should look like this (this will be the head, seen from the back).

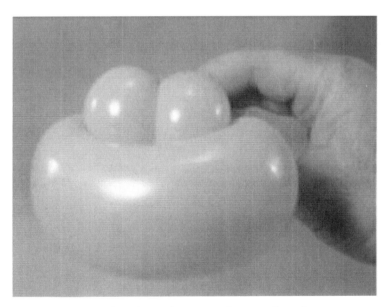

16- And here is the head, seen from the front.

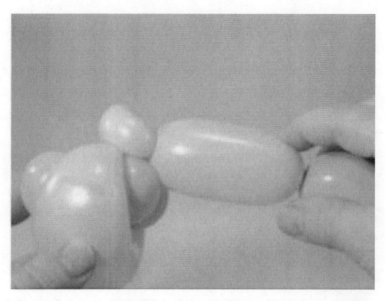

17- Next, form a bubble about three fingers wide.

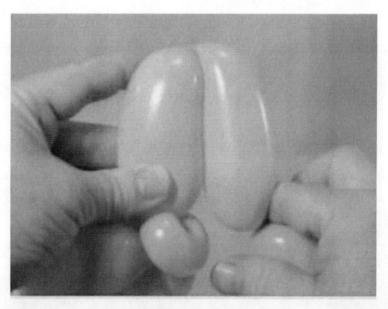

18- Form a second bubble making sure it's the same size as the first, and bring them together...

19- press them together at the base, and twist them together several times to block them together.

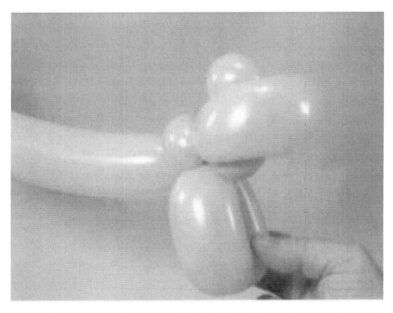

20- Our frog now has a whole head and two front legs.

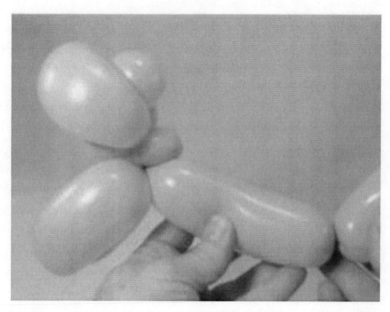

21- Make a longer bubble for the body.

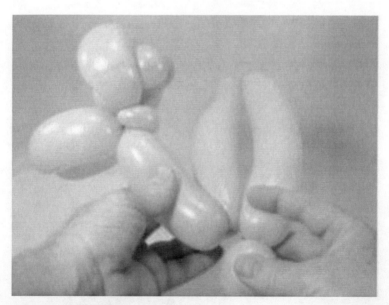

22- Then, with the remaining length of balloon, make two big bubbles of the same length (the hind legs), followed by a final, small, round bubble.

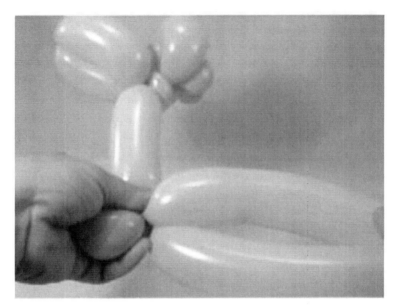

23- Press the hind legs together at the base and twist them together several times to block them together.

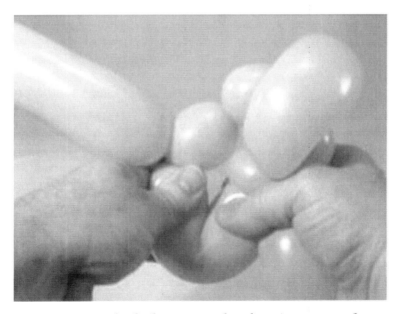

24- Give a rounded shape to the frog's stomach.

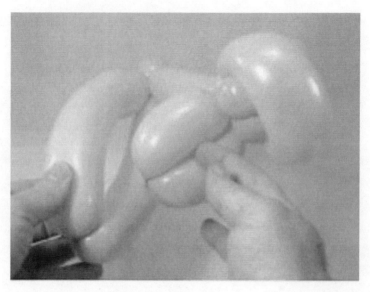

25- Now you need to insert the short front legs between the long hind legs.

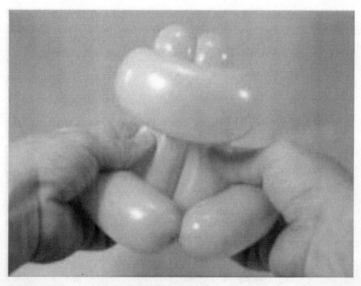

26- Widen the gap between the hind legs if need be, but not too much. There still needs to be enough tension to keep the front legs in place.

27- Here is our little frog with no drawing on it.

28- And here it is, drawn on with a black felt-tip marker and a few touches of white.

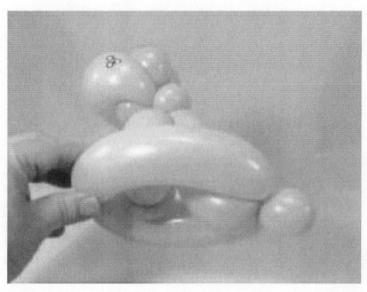

29- The body can be positioned in several ways. It can be pushed between the two hind legs...

30- or, conversely, left to stick out which gives the frog an arched back. The back can also be shorter, it's at your discretion.

31- The result!

Pattern 3 – The Tiger

Step-By-Step Photo Guide

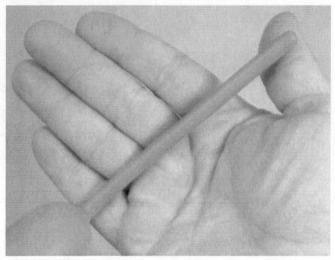

1- Inflate a balloon leaving a margin at the end of slightly more than the width of a hand. Then tie the knot.

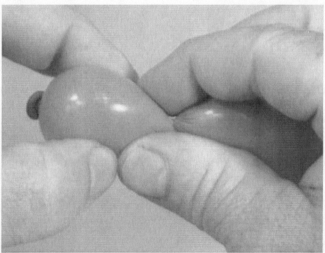

2- Starting from the knotted end, make a first, well-rounded bubble.

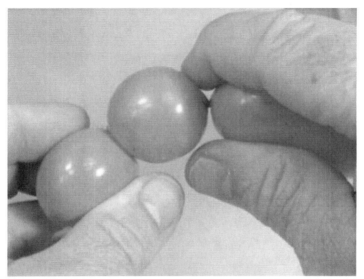

3- Make a second, identical bubble, following the first.

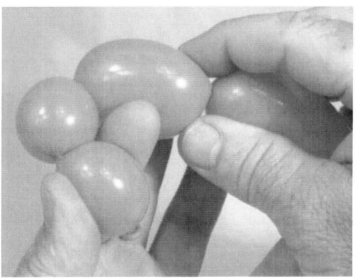

4- Follow these with a third bubble, this time a little wider than the first two.

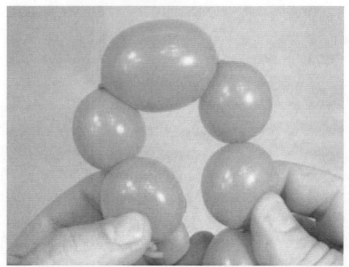

5- To finish the row of bubbles, make two more bubbles identical to the first two. If need be, review how to make a row of bubbles without them getting undone.

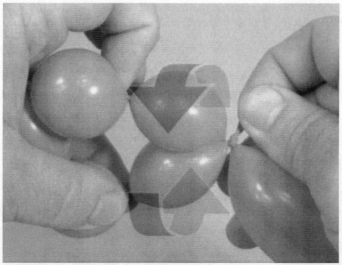

6- Holding the knot to the base of the row of bubbles, twist the bubbles several times together around their base to block them.

7- You should get a shape similar to this one.

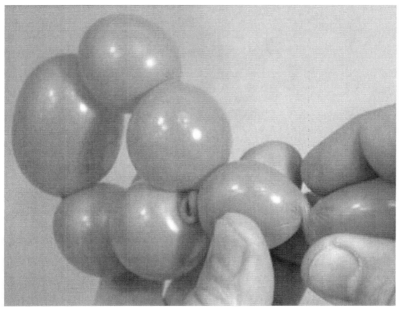

8- Form another well-rounded bubble,

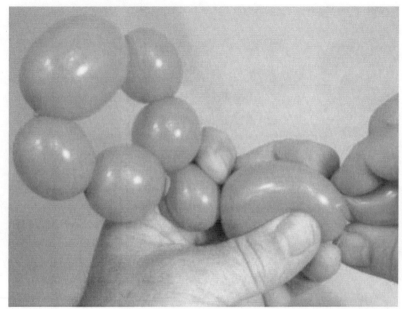

9- then, a second bubble following it, a little longer than the first (about double).

10- You should now have a shape similar to this one.

11- Feed the new little bubble, then the larger one, through the loop formed by the first row of bubbles.

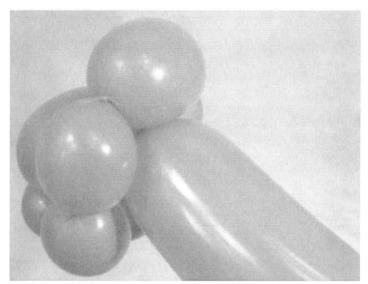

12- The fold between the last big bubble and the remaining portion of balloon should fall into place naturally to form a right angle with with the first large bubble.

13- Front view. With a little imagination, you can already start to see the tiger's cheeks, its forehead, its muzzle, and its ears sticking out a little on either side.

14- In fact, take the bubble representing the right ear (or the left ear if you are left-handed). And pinch it...

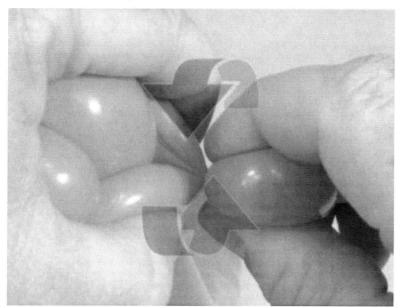

15- to make a **'pinch-twist'**.

16- Here is the first ear of the tiger.

17- Next turn the head to pinch the bubble representing the left ear (or right ear if you are left-handed and you started on the other side).

18- Make another **'pinch-twist'**.

19- Now, here is the head of our tiger with both of its ears well shaped.

20- For the rest, it's exactly the same body as **the little doggy's**. Form a round bubble for the neck (it can be slightly oval, but make sure it isn't too long!)

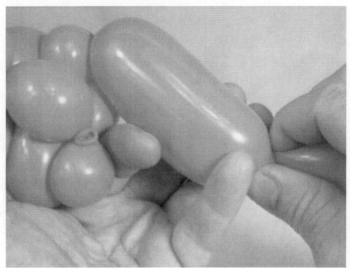

21- Holding the head so the bubble for the neck won't get undone, form a long bubble about three fingers wide to make the tiger's first leg.

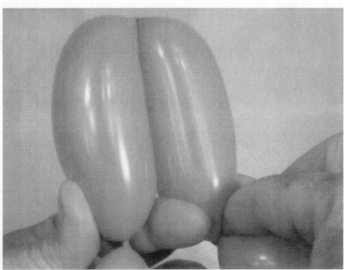

22- Still holding the head, twist the remaining portion of balloon against the first leg to form a second leg of equal length to the first.

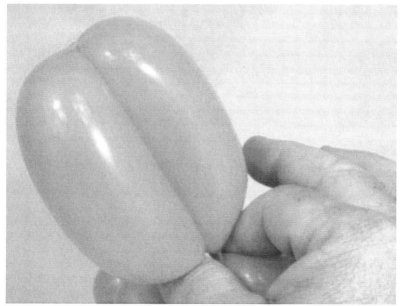

23- Firmly pinch them together at their base.

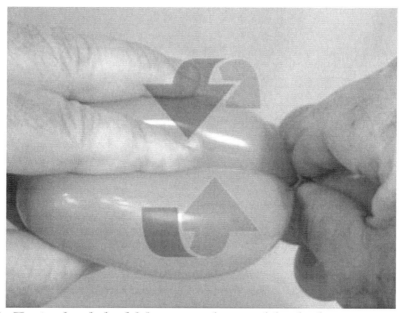

24- Twist both bubbles together to block them.

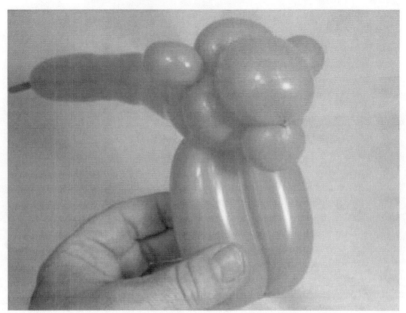

25- Our little tiger is starting to take shape.

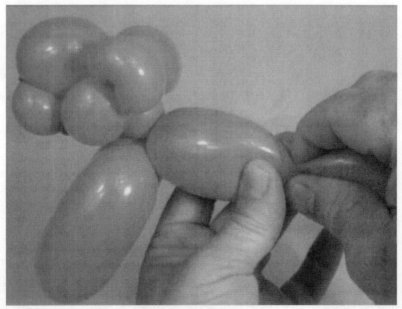

26- Make another oval bubble for the stomach.

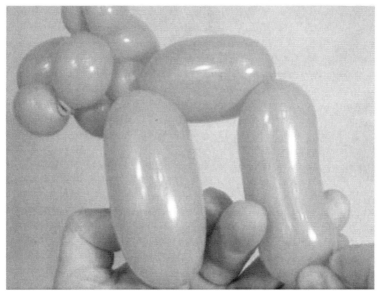

27- Make another oval bubble following it, making sure it's the same size as the front legs.

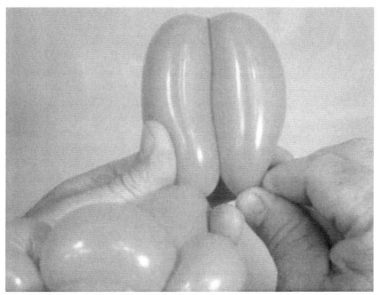

28- Then one last bubble for the second hind leg. You will have to make sure it's the same length as the previous bubble.

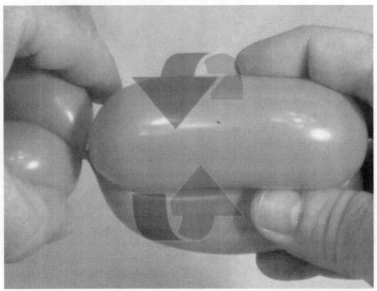

29- Pinch the hind legs together at their base and twist them together to wedge them in place.

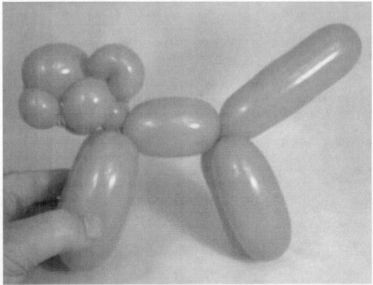

30- Now, here is our little tiger. Let's perfect a few details to make it a little less stiff and a bit more natural-looking.

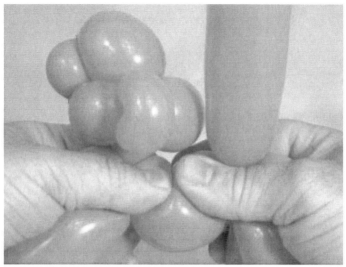

31- Hold both ends of the stomach bubble and **gently** move them back and forth, to rub them **gently** against each other at the center of the bubble.

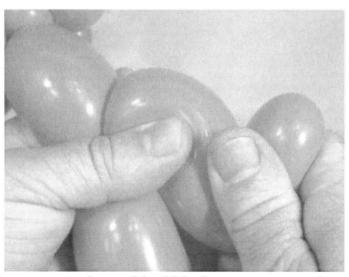

32- Next, press the tail bubble between your hands, to form an **S** shape, and like previously, rub **gently** at the folds of the **S**.

33- With **curved shapes**, our little tiger looks much better now, doesn't it? The thing have to do now is to draw a few features on it to bring it to life.

And that's it for today.

Pattern 4 - Tux The Penguin

Step-By-Step Photo Guide

1- Inflate a white balloon leaving a margin at the end of slightly more than the width of a hand. Then tie the knot.

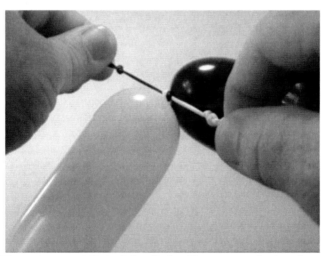

2- Do likewise with a black balloon and tie the knotted end of each balloon together.

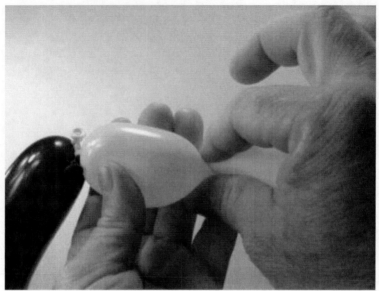

3- With the white balloon, make a first oval bubble about three fingers wide.

4- Make a second, identical bubble, following the first.

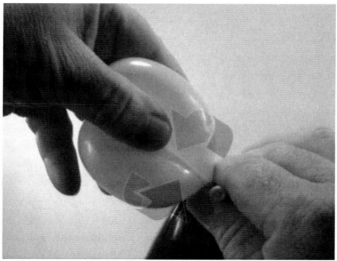

5- Twist the bubbles several times around their base to keep them in place.

6- Roll the black balloon along the groove located between the two white bubbles. In this way, shape a wide black loop and bring its base to the base of the two white bubbles.

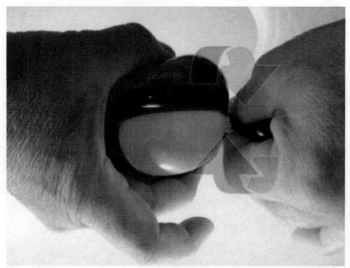

7- Twist the two white bubbles and the black loop several times around their base to keep them in place.

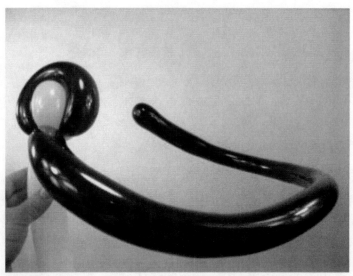

8- **Push the air** to the end of the remaining portion of black balloon (don't bother with the remaining portion of white balloon for the moment), you should get a shape similar to this one.

9- Make a zigzag with the rest of the black balloon so that the last segment is slightly longer than the first two. Make a mental note of the position of each of the two bends thus formed.

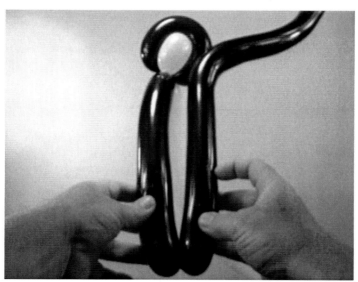

10- Make a first long bubble at the first bend formed by the zigzag.

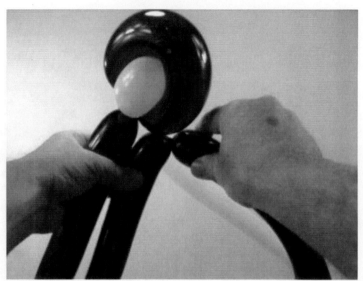

11- Then make a second long bubble, identical to the first, normally it should fall more or less at the second bend formed by the zigzag.

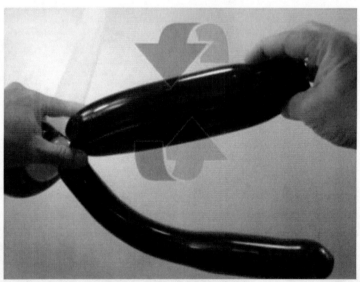

12- Twist the two large black bubbles around their base several times to block them at the base of Tux's head.

13- You should now have a shape resembling this one, with at the center, under the head, the two wings 've been created (the two long black bubbles).

14- With what's left of the black balloon, make a bubble that's shorter than the previous two. Doing so you will also get one final bubble that should be wedged between the two wings.

15- Then roll this last bubble several times between the wings to keep everything firmly in place. You can now make out Tux's head, wings, back and tail.

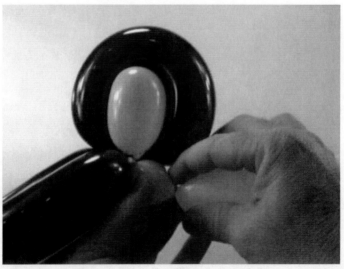

16- Go back to the white balloon and form a small, round bubble at the base of Tux's head.

17- Make this bubble into **a pinch-twist** which will enable us to keep Tux's head firmly in place on top of its back and shoulders (or rather its back and wings).

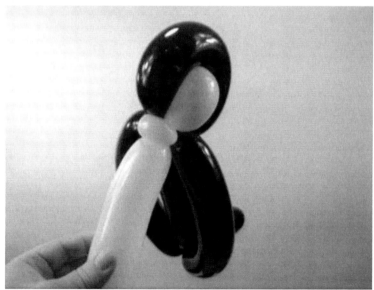

18- Notice that the rest of the white balloon is naturally located under the pinch-twist.

19- You will have to feed it through to the other side, so that you can use it to make Tux's belly.

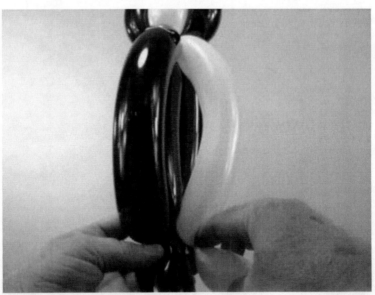

20- **Push the air** in the white balloon a bit towards the end, and shape a large bubble for the belly which should look a little rounded.

21- Then finish **pushing the air all the way to the end of the white balloon** so that there is no remaining length of empty balloon.

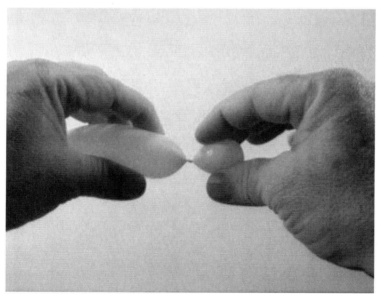

22- Make a small bubble at the tip of the white balloon.

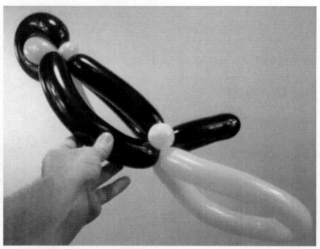

23- Then wedge the small white bubble into the joint common to the base of the wings, the base of the back, and the tail. It doesn't matter which side the bubble is sticking out from for now. Having done this, you get a large **loop**.

24- Divide one big loop into two smaller loops. To do this, twist the large white loop into two equal parts and take note of the central mark.

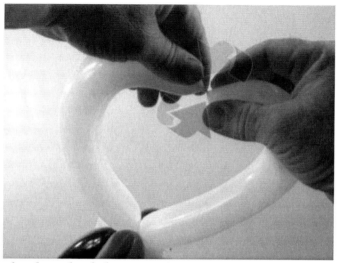

25- At the level of this mark, press the balloon to form two large bubbles then hold one of the bubbles firmly in one hand while twisting the other bubble around its base with the other hand, to divide the loop into two equal parts.

26- This way, you get two distinct bubbles. Now let's see how to turn both of them into loops.

27- It's very simple! All you need to do is bring the creases formed at the ends of each bubble together, and thus naturally shape two new (smaller) loops.

28- Hold one of the loops firmly in one hand while twisting the other loop around its base with your other hand to keep them both in place.

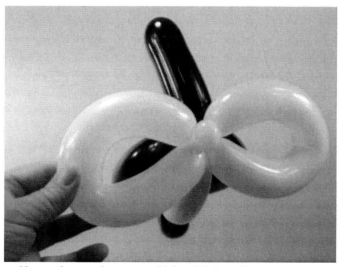

29- Finally, place the small bubble, that you had set aside, right between the two loops. You have just made two wide, webbed feet, on which Tux can now stand securely.

30- You are almost finished. All that's left now is the beak! For this, **very lightly** inflate a small round balloon, preferably yellow.

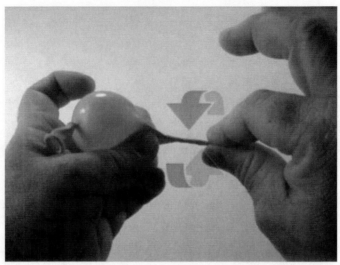

31- Press on the tip of the balloon and, gripping the latex, twist the tip a little so that the air leaves it completely and pushes against the knotted end of the balloon.

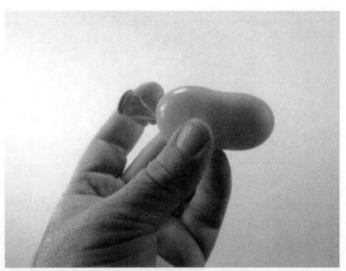

32- Gently let go of the latex to enable the air to come back gradually into the balloon, which should now be elongated or at the very least oval.

33- Wedge the knotted end of the beak at the base of the head. Lastly, draw on the eyes, and **round out** the shapes of Tux's wings, back and stomach to put the finishing touches on this sculpture.

And that's all there is to it!

Pattern 5 - The Giraffe

Step-By-Step Photo Guide

1- Inflate a balloon leaving a margin of about 5 fingers in width.

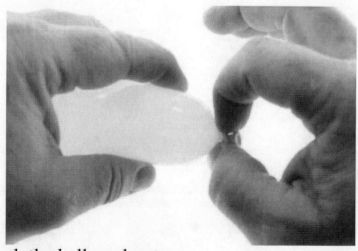

2- Grab the balloon knot.

3- Pull on the knot to free up an extra length of latex.

4- Press the balloon,

5- so the air will flow back towards the knot and fill up the short length of latex that has just been freed up.

6- Carry out an initial **control of air pressure**.

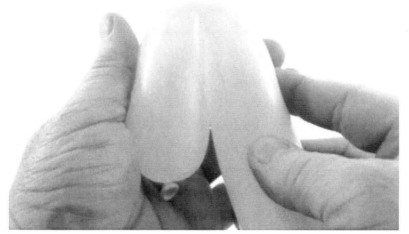

7- Bend the balloon about 3 fingers away from the knot.

8- Create **an acute angle** at the level of this bend.

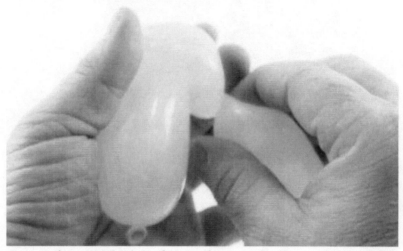

9- Once the angle has been formed, close the bubble just below it.

10- The idea is to get an offset bubble.

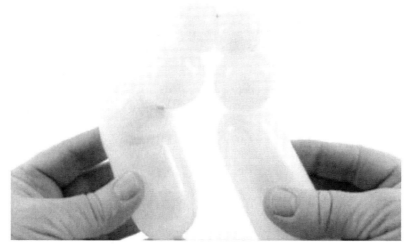

11- Next, make 4 bubbles in a row. The first and fourth ones will be wider than the second and third ones.

12- Block the row of 4 bubbles at their base.

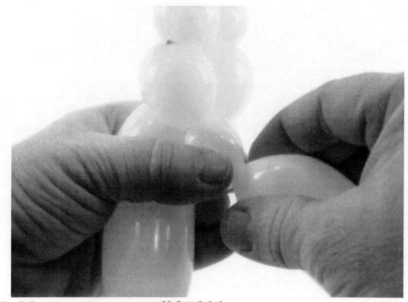

13- Next create a small bubble,

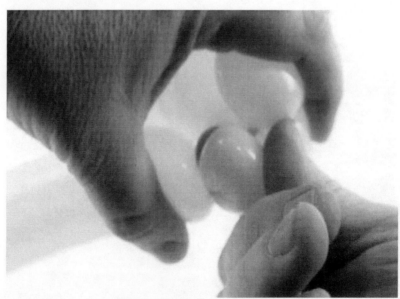

14- and turn this small bubble into a **pinch-twist,**

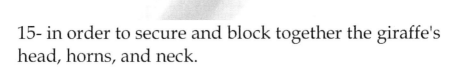

15- in order to secure and block together the giraffe's head, horns, and neck.

16- Divide the remaining segment of balloon into 3 roughly equal parts, just to mark where the first third ends.

17- Create **an acute angle** at the first bend (at the third of the remaining portion of balloon).

18- You should get this shape.

19- Close the bubble just beneath the angle.

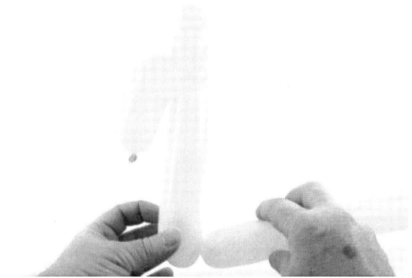

20- Once again, the idea is to get an offset bubble (which will enable us to easily and naturally have the neck pointing upwards).

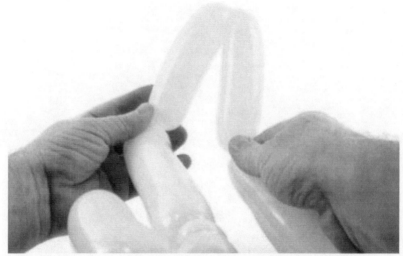

21- Make 1 more bubble about a quarter of the length of the remaining segment of balloon, then a second bubble of the same length, just after the first one, and block them together.

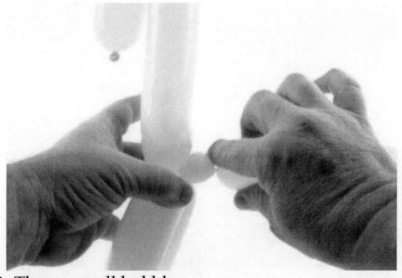

22- Then a small bubble,

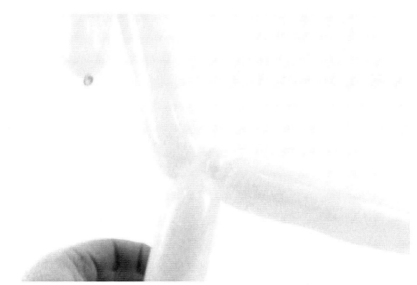

23- which you will turn into **a pinch-twist**, in order to consolidate the articulation between the neck and the front legs.

24- Carry out one last **air pressure control** so that there's no room left in the remaining portion of balloon.

25- Divide the remaining portion of balloon into two parts, the last part being the shorter one. Then press these two large bubbles together, to create a crease just before the tip of the last bubble.

26- Twist the two bubbles together at the base of this crease.

27- Doing so, you get the last two legs of the giraffe, its short tail, and belly, all in a single movement.

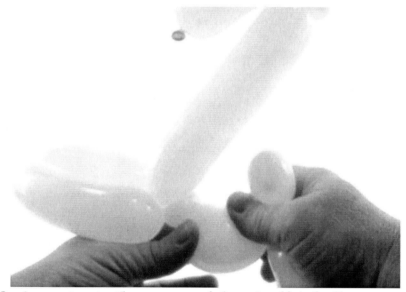

28- **Accentuate the curve** of the giraffe's belly.

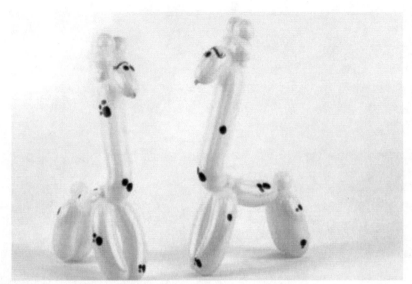

29- Draw a few lines for the face and spots... and there you have it!

Made in United States
North Haven, CT
11 October 2023